MOVING LANDSCAPE

Moving Landscape
is the twenty-third volume
in the *Essential Poets* Series
published by
Guernica Editions.

PASQUALE VERDICCHIO

MOVING LANDSCAPE

Guernica Editions

Some of these poems have appeared in *From an Island, Student Oracles,* and *Whetstone.*

Infinite thanks to my family, Liesbeth, and Antonio.

Guernica Editions, P.O. Box 633, Station N.D.G., Montréal (Québec)
Canada H3A 3R1

Canadian Cataloguing in Publication Data

Verdicchio, Pasquale, 1954 — Moving Landscape

(Essential poets; 23) Poems
ISBN 0-919349-59-5 bound. — ISBN 0-919349-58-7

I. Title.   II. Series

PS8593.E692M6 1985   C811'.54   C85-090099-9
PR9199.3.V47M6 1985

Contents

DESK CALENDAR

What did we do when we loosened this earth from its sun? Whither does it now move? Whither do we move? Away from all suns? Do we not dash on unceasingly? Backwards, sideways, forward, in all directions? Is there still an above and below? Do we not stray, as through infinite nothingness? Does not empty space breathe upon us? Has it not become colder? Does not night come on continually, darker and darker?

Nietzsche
The Gay Science

Red-Winged Blackbird

Wind. Wind
and wings of birds.
A red-winged blackbird
sparks against the sky
and green shrubs;
comes to rest in the safety
of calls that break
against our words,
clear and intelligible words,
and light the evening
with the fire of meaning.

Letter

A blue envelope stained by foreign fingers;
in one corner a far land's pride.

The wind has carried you far
and your feet
have touched many soils.
And when your memory permits,
pen in one hand
and all you have gathered
tight in the other,
you send me
what your sun-dark hands have held.

Another place name fallen
to the page, its letters broken
to mean a thousand words.
Rain will wash the blue letter tiles
to white in time;
time will change the blue words
to yellow... on this page.

You have sold yourself.
The bones, in the sun
they so much desired,
pass time to white and dust;
these I will use
to make more names of places
which may not even be.

Imperfect Shadows

Waking as darkness falls
hard on the spine of rivers;
grit between my teeth, the moon
pulls blood to my head, eyes bloodshot.
Where was this birth conceived?
Water softly touches the perimeter of thoughts
as I lay face down in thawing winter.
There is nowhere to walk,
nowhere to stop.
There is only moonlight in water,
only dirt and mud and weeds,
hiding imperfect shadows
too stubborn to drown.

Fish

1
Moon tears in sea skin
converse creatures
walled by currents
scale senses

gills, fins motion secrets

2
Hovering in mid-water free
flight in denseness
nothing holding to this
depth or that
savouring each movement

3
New phosphorescence
tapering into fin lobe
vanishes with darkness

4
The only trace
a fish leaves is one
imprinted in water past
and carved from water-logged wood

Mexico

1

A carnation lights the way
to words we once thought spoken.
They are scattered as old petals
seeking recollection of the shape.
Fire crown of heliotropic transfer;
a warm face staring up in self-proclamation.

2

The wash on the roof sways back and forth
remembering the movement of bodies.
Night listens for the last door to close
and footsteps to climb the stair.
In a dark room a bright star moves
to invisible lips belonging to a man
who continually listens for daybreak.

3

A glass of wax:
offering to unknown faces
that hold secrets we would like to glimpse.
Wax, hard and cold;
fingers have left their mark
for the gods.
Wax: soul in solid state
rememberance for the forgetful.

4
The tombs of kings
with jade skulls and shell
eyes staring into empty promises.
Only priests knew how to deceive
both men and gods;
their names still repeated
by the steps of pyramids.

5
"An invisible landscape
conditions the visible one."
A thousand wells touch water,
move upward. Where gods are left a choice
they inhabit everything.

Scars

At night no movement is apparent
unless a time exposure constructs luminous paths.

An eye looking at the photograph
discerns a center where none exists:
deceptive truth of undifferentiated light.

Night Song

Lyrics strained by air — warts on trees,
tree-frogs resume their song cycle.
His eyes look out,
envelop dark branches,
become fruits unwilling to fall
to invisible ground.

Between the Desert

The sea. Not the sea.
Music reaches out from towers:
notes reflected in the eyes of women.
Desires, already memories,
encrusted with onyx and agate.
A traveller arrives, misunderstands
the redundance that fills his eyes:
always leaving, always returning,
he finds himself between the desert.

Smooth Stones

Water breaking against rock is not light
though it shines. And stones become
accustomed to smooth feet, become smooth themselves.
It is the wind that talks through stones,
leaves carvings to be read.

Couple in the South

Warmth through his hands touches
to bring her closer. She sees the harbour
float at his back; the sun and his colour
repeated on rooftops. Boats with no sails
wave their masts as bony fingers urging
"No." He looks out of the frame in defiance
and keeps her close. No-one can enter,
no-one else belongs in this dream he has
built for her.

Pasqua

Red roofs colour the view:
planes reaching a common focus.
The horizon is invisible behind city noise;
swallows circle, attempt to fill space.
When the purple cloth is removed
the eyes have disappeared.

Barcelona

The door of Hostel Marmo greets us
with a cracked smile.
The hall
stairs
small and winding
cold
as is the room.
Night follows us in.

Morning reveals early Spanish furniture.
The post office across the way has begun
juggling mail. On the ledge
of the next building, a pigeon,
dying, does not notice a cat
moving in on him.

There is no flamenco echoing in these streets anymore:
the accent is all that is left.
Picasso women, white powdered faces and twisted eyes,
stare and follow their noses up alleys.
Black kerchiefs, dark eyes, *boinas*, and white shirts
run for trains leaving early. At every corner
armed guards protect democracy with their mustaches.

The port is the only way out:
Columbus stands in the square and points the way.
Everyone fixes their eyes on the invisible dreamland.
In the backstreets roams America.
Jeans, tee-shirts, and an occasional O.K. rise up
between buildings out of the exhaust.

Columbus turns around.

Funeral for a Fisherman

They wait till the sun is out of striking range
before venturing into wounded streets
to bring the man down from where the screams came —
his wife's terror at his decision.
Now they take him through cooler streets
along bowed bare heads to the small square
by the docks that were his life,
up again, through the quickness of town,
along the path we take each day to the beach,
to the cemetery which waits — already feeling
the coldness of another breath.

Ancestors

1
Because we were the dreams
which ancestors carved in stone
and described in jewels
we are now lost and confused
as to whether these lives are our own
or if they will cease with another's waking.

2
The blueness of the sky not as immediate
as the horizon pretends it to be,
whiteness shows through
where the artist overlooked space.
Incomplete mosaic of our lives
betrays the subtle equilibrium.

3
Arms with bracelets of gold wound
around blood of their wrists.
Arms of Etruscan figures
whose loins spawned words gold and silver
from the sperm of mystery which spilled
into the Arno and down to the sea.
Only tombs of anagrams are left
telling of freedom in the guise of figurines:
their eyes closed in damp excavations,
arms embracing the memory
we hold of them.

4
Ancestors invented reigns
for their imagination
and promised lands they were
unable to keep; these
we now suffer as beliefs.

Woman at the Well

She said the well wall was low,
she had to get close to the edge
to pull up the bucket; there was no wheel.
She said the well was deep,
as deep as the earth looks
from atop the highest mountain,
and the depth called her name.
The flashing reflections she did not recognize
shattered images playing below.

When her feet broke the surface
the surge of coolness made her forget
the sun on the back of her head.
Dark cool dark and smooth caresses
flowing up her legs against her body,
she opened her mouth for the kiss —
and water became her.
Her eyes melted into all the images.

Air, forgetting her standing memory,
began to fill the emptiness.

Ritual

Thinking himself unseen, the man
at the end of the street
makes love to a setting sun.
The curtain on his door whispers
its movement in the wind. His
hands reach high into branches,
spill silent into the air:
a conversation,
a plea for nothing more
than a repetition of the ritual.

Kafka: House in the Country

Walked a long way, a very long way,
to find deserts desert enough;
starlit nights to feel the wind
forced down between light spaces.

I rush toward things feeling their movement
in my veins, my heart pumping rapids
rushing to fill that space the river leaves
as it moves toward the sea.
Silent waters run,
I am not present to hear
words they suggest.
Out here there are no spaces
for silence to fall into
and so many crevices for me
to crawl around in. Ottla, the house
in the country, a Chinese box
I lock myself into.
What could I know of life in a city
where I keep changing into little animals
everyone would rather see dead.

Ottla, betrothed and sister,
you are the sign of shelter;
your home the sign of you.
"I need your past"
to build your life,
the life that complements my walks
as I fall silent
with words that run for cover.
Above and below words

there is no room for escape:
no wings to fly.
I work my way underneath on hands and knees
muddied in the residue of ink.

Le Tombeau de Dante

Calle del Carmen:

in one corner of a courtyard
looking away from the crowded street
a white face of stone.

The grave in Ravenna a diversion.

How could a man die
after a voyage such as his.
Time is now spent searching
for secrets in a land
where temples were built
and sacrifices made to the light
he once saw and attempted to lock
in his words of heaven and hell.

Mario Fallani's Icarus

His Icarus falls among foliage.
Naked he walks
unhurt the canvas gardens.
An image blurred by gusts of air
forcing against flesh.
Invisible in mirrors he sits
at a table contemplating
the reflection of his eyes undefined.
Eyes betray thoughts of water,
his hands pearled with drops.
Icarus — his image without death —
talks a language of flight
whose words lightly leave their colour
before rising to their rightful place.

Coelacanth

for Bert Schierbeek

He grew up in the country;
his poetry smelled ancient,
of Devonian strata.
I don't remember his name
but his smile is hard
to forget. We left him extinct
until his wrinkles, cycloid
scales, broke over us.
(He was re-discovered living in the sea
off southeastern Africa.)
The found fossil verses were small
in stature, and deceiving.
His writhing body, wrapped in age,
and the name he dropped on the table
told of his resurrection.
Missing-link polemics were all
that held him back.
Now, his old words are ready:
mute fish movement translated into phrases.

Artaud and Nobody

During his great voyage
he changed his name to reflect
the seas he had travelled,
names of his experience.
To everyone he came to be
know as what the one-eyed visionary
had called him: Nobody.
Nobody returned home
to find he had never been there
and his name, usurped by words,
found its way across centuries
becoming over and over the traveller:
man searching and finding himself
tied against songs of mermaids
and temptation. He became once and again
others, became the name,
so that the man had to take another.
While his name walked through
the pages of Ireland the man wandered
aimless and lost, then found himself
mentioned by the tortured mind of Art
who wrote to his friend Anne:
"Give my address to Nobody in Paris.
This is very important!"

A City

A dream led men to build a city
of tangle-yarn streets which wait
the bare foot of a woman. These same men hope
to stop her as she passes.

Each man runs his own pursuit
and rearranges spaces to deceive the running.
Streets they have built are now their world;
a maze of changes, dreams, and chase.
Arched doorways waiting for an entrance
look down concrete steps to reach the main square
where now and then men gather
for more strategy, more building.
Other men come day by day,
all led by a passing woman:
streets and doorways locked in their heads,
waiting to be the ones
to catch elusive footsteps.

The dream changes constantly;
the woman passes unnoticed
while men argue as to which dream
she will pass through.

MOVING LANDSCAPE

Plus d'un, comme moi sans doute, écrivent pour n'avoir plus de visage. Ne me demandez pas qui je suis et ne me dites pas de rester le même...

Foucault
L'Archéologie du savoir

Ein Zeichen sind wir, deutungslos, Schmerzlos sind wir und haben fast Die Sprache in der Fremde verloren.

Hölderlin
"Mnemosyne"

I am the only man missing
from the landscape
of a ready-made history.
The face in morning mirrors
wears a name
subtracted from me.
(Subtract everything.
Nothing must be left over
for something to be a part of.
Subtract from the whole
until everything is alone;
things can be seen as they move
against each other,
for each other,
in each other.
I am subtracting myself from the scene
to see my function as an absence.)

Every word I add is a leaving:
this city, not my city, any city
built up of many departures,
always completed in thought
as round trips.

There is a metamorphosis
others enact on my body
as I try to put distance between
with words.
It is never clear
who is the hunter
in worn skins.
The chase renews itself
with the threat of an end.
Masks exhaust themselves,

unclear physiognomy.
Eyes have always known
the same landscape.

Interchangeable masks;
underneath that which does not change:
veiled eyes,
the mouth, a bottomless well
waiting for the stone.
Words in their hiding places
wait for the face to change
into something other than the real.

There is no language without deceipt.
A grammar of bodies and images
grown out of false form.
It begins here,
and it must go on deceiving
to give words a chance to move
layer over layer.
They contain much like water
contains, is contained,
envelops, is displaced,
where form is content,
content form.
No sounds mark the air,
all lost in transformation;
escape
only possible in silence.

I have been far forever now:
night is tired
of stripping herself for others,
her writing black on black.

I hear her compose,
with raucous voice,
the long forgotten
progression of memories.

Between lands lie water
and islands,
fragments of renewal
(since no image of me remains
on your dear land
or on mine).

Something remains of the voice,
cannot touch it — death has not
touched it —
and it makes its way
over oyster-rough sand,
listens
to whispering crabs:
signs of movement.

It rises and winds
around tree tops bending.
Distance moves into slopes;
spaces among scarse vegetation
gather magic,
and even though it seems to have stopped,
to have fallen victim, it climbs
toward a sky undefined by treeline.

Eyes move never lost,
never cheated by the absent limit —
behind the forest pine-needle floor,

high ceilings
frescoed with strokes of cedar.

Falling asleep, thinking of death,
my mother suddenly screaming
something important,
something she had longed to say.
And then death.

Dance in the dark.
Words exorcised from vegetation.

Over the fire
(of hemmorage)
pages burn.
Black words become darker;
everything becomes night.

She closes her eyes
moving like trees do
just before breaking to the wind.

And night is the material
from which to construct poems.

Holding the hand of death,
feeding her patiently, she cannot
move in her chair.

One by one
making small talk
to avoid looking into her eyes,
to keep her occupied,

keep her in that body
which knows her waiting,
keep her mind off the rest of us
sitting around drinking,
keep a smile somewhere behind her lips
and her hands held tightly together.

Destiny: the horizon is birds.
Stains become burdens to the sky.

Our fingertips blood-stained
feathers in our hands;
travelling without wings over water.

Promises upwelling
to wash salt from our skin.

Destiny: the surface is
dense to touch, resembles sky.

We break
into the solidity of meeting.

A polarized circle moves,
submerged, which way
is it reflection or opaqueness?

Destiny: our end is
caught between ambiguity of surfaces.

This
not an anchor
to be carried down
into depth. This —
a stone, pumice,
with a memory of fire,
burning motion
above tongue-tied ruins.

Printed in Canada
at Les Ateliers Graphiques Marc Veilleux Inc.
in August 1985